WHO AM I

I am who God says I am, I was born of a woman, shaped and mold after God's own image. I was born to be a helper to man, not a slave. God took the rib from man's side and closed the side back up and with the rib he formed woman, because she was formed from 'man's side, this explains why a man leaves his father and mother and is joined to his wife, who am I, I am who God says I am born into a world of sin only to be saved by the goodness of our Lord and Savior Jesus the Christ, who am I? I am a servant of the king, I must live a life pleasing to my Heavenly Father. A good reputation is more valuable than the most perfume, the word says mere dreaming of nice things is foolish, it's like chasing the wind, all things are decided by fate, it was known long ago what each man or woman would be, there's no arguing with God about our destiny I am who God says I am, In this silly life, I have seen everything including the fact that some of the good die young and some of the wicked live on and on, I'm going to live the life that God gave me, to be pleasing in his sight, to tackle whatever task that comes before me, to fear God, then and only then shall I expect to receive my blessings. I am who God says I am, I will love the Lord with all my heart, soul, mind and strength so that I may live again. Who am I, I am the woman at the well, who left her water pot and went into the City and told the men to come, see a man that told me all things that ever I done. Who am I? I am Mary and Martha weeping for Lazarus. Who am I, I'm Naomi and her daughter In-law trying to survive, who am I, I'm Sarah saying Abraham is my brother, Who am I, I am Mary the mother of Jesus, following her son unto death".

Who am I, I'm Anna, Miriam, Deborah, Huldah, and the four daughters of phillip, who was given the gift of prophecy. I am who God says I am. Im Hannah crying out to the Lord to bless her with a child, and if he bless her she will give him back to the Lord. Who am I, I'm Peters mother sick with a fever, who was healed by just a touch of the masters hand. Who am I, I am who Gods says I am, I'm the daughter of the king, born for a purpose, to bring truth to the world, Telling others of Jesus love, who am I, I am who God says I am, I'm grace, mercy, righteous, cherished, treasured, a conqueror, love, joy, peace, and happiness. If anybody ask you who I am, tell them, I'm not all that I can be, I'm not what I should be, but I'm better than I was. Who am I, I am a laborer of the King I

Work daily for him so that my work will endure forever, Who am I, I am the daughter of Annie Bell. I walk by faith not by sight. Who am I, I am woman redeemed.

Dear God

Today is the hardest day of my life, the day that I was born my mom took her last breath and went to sleep in Heaven. My heart hurt's so bad, I know she is in a better place, but I want her back with me. Mom was my rock, my joy, my friend and hero. The day she left she took a piece of my heart with her. Lord help me, give me the strength to go on, my life will never be the same. My children and grandchildren are broken, they had nothing but unconditional love for there Grama. Lord please bless my husband he loved and cared for my mom as if she was his. We need your help Lord come see about your children. You said in your word that you would not put more on us than we can bear, I need you to hide me under your wings, be my shield and buckler during these hard difficult days ahead. Be my light when darkness surrounds me, hold my hand Lord and walk with me, you said that you will give us the desires of thine heart if we delight -ourselves in you. I'm standing on your promises Lord. I'm watching the undertaker wrap my mom in a blanket, my heart is beating so fast, Lord I want to stop him but I can't, I hear myself crying out, saying I want my mom back, I need her, my son is holding me tight, I'm screaming for you Lord to bring her back like you did Larazus, I'm not ready for her to go just yet, I was moving in slow motion is she really gone or am I dreaming, help us Lord. The glue that kept us together is gone. In order for us to see mom again, we will have to live for Christ, the work mom did on earth is her reward in Heaven. Mom gave me life on July 19th and what's so amazing is that you called her name on the same day she gave birth to me, She hung around for my special day, sleep on mom take your rest I'll see you in the morning.

Dear God

In all thy ways I will acknowledge you and let you direct my paths, giving thanks to you waking me up another day, thanks for sending your Angels to camp around our door all night long, keeping us safe in our home, you kept the thieves and robbers away, you woke us up to see another day for that I say thank you, Father bless those that are sick in the hospitals, in convalescing home and those in their own homes that are sick, touch them with your healing power, raise them back up from their sick beds if it's your will. Lord I pray for this world, our economy, bless our President as he tries to lead this country, bless those that are fighting for us and those that served our country for our protection, bless them and their families. Lord I pray for those without shelter, without food, without any financial support at all, bless them Lord. I pray that the loss will seek your word, turn from their wicked ways and learn of you and your goodness and mercy. Help me not to be so quickly to judge others, because if it had not been for your grace and mercy there goes I. Give me the strength to continue to learn about you, to continue to seek after righteousness, to study your word, in Jesus name I pray Amen.

Dear God

It feels as though I'm walking around in fog, all I want to do is sleep so that I won't have to face another day, I can't leave the house, I'm crying all day I need you to help me Lord, take my pain away, give me the ability to accept your will, I know that absent from the body is present with you Lord, That mom is sleeping until that great day when you return, but tell my heart that. I can hear mom saying it's time for her to rest and for me to live so that I can see her again, that's she's living in her new home that you prepared for her, she's saying the streets are paved with Gold, there's no sickness or death up there, that everyday feels like Sunday, that you are feeding them with manner from on high. I hear mom saying keep praying daughter the prayers of the righteous availeth much, God hears you and he has you in the palm of his hand. I hear mom saying look to the Holy Spirit to comfort you, That you can do all things through Christ which strengtheneth you. God you are my light and my salvation with you on my side I shall not fear any evil because you are a very present help in times of sorrow and trouble. Lord you are truly my prince of peace, thanks for drying on tcross for me and others. I will let your light shine amongst people that they may learn of your wondrous works. In Jesus name I pray Amen.

Kathleen Copeland

Dear God

We know that all things work together for good to them that love you, and who are called according to his purpose. Lord thanks for creating the Heavens and the Earth, and everything that is in it. Adam and Eve caused sin to appear in the world but you blessed us anyway. Help me to strive to live Holy, to do what is acceptable, your perfect will. Bless the sick and shut in, put a fence around our children, Keep them safe from Satan, he's running rampant in this earth, he has our children killing each other, he has them doing all kinds of drugs, He has them worshiping him instead of you, Let them remember to obey their parents so that there days upon this Earth may be long. Lord help us to teach our children that it is a privilege to carry all our troubles and burdens to in prayer and believe that you hear them and will answer them. Lord I know you will step in right when the Devil thinks he's won, change my tomorrow today, life happens at your speed. Father God bless all that stands in the need of a blessing today, in Jesus name I pray Amen.

Dear God

I will bless the Lord at all times and his praise shall continually be in my mouth. God I was born unto sin, but I was shaped by your word to live a Godly life. I try not to worry about tomorrow because I know you hold the future in your hands. Lord bless my household, keep us grounded, and keep our minds stayed on you. Lord continue to fight my battles, the emptiness that I'm feeling right now replace it with love. Give me wisdom to learn your word as I study daily. Lord I'm grateful for a Godly husband, who studies reads your word daily. Bless him with understanding of your word. Lord I'm praying for those that know you but is not trying to come and worship with you, give me encouraging word to say kindly that you need to come and hear the the word that the Shepherd has to feed his church. Help me to be a witness to others that they need to hear what "thus says the Lord". At some point and time they will have to call on the name of Jesus to come and help them. Lord I need to tell others that when they are feeling weak, weary and torn all they need to do is call on the name of Jesus and he will come and see about his children, he will pick you up turn you around and place your feet back on solid ground. Lord I want to see your light ever shinning in my heart, you are the Author and finisher of my faith, you are the light for my pathway, you are Alpha and Omega, the beginning and the end. Lord please be a Rock for me in a weary land, my bright and shining star, you are the Air that I breath, you feeds me with manna from on high, thank you Lord,

——————————————— *Kathleen Copeland*

you are my doctor in a sick room, my lawyer in a court room. Father God, I can hear my Grama saying call him up and tell him what you want, his line is never busy, he's always on time, he's omnipotent, omnipresent, just tell him what you want, what you need, believe it in your heart and you will receive it. Jesus I can hear you calling me Servant, Servant, my good and faithful child, I heard your cry, doors are open for you in my father's house, I prepared a place for you, there are many mansions up here, welcome to your new home in my father's house. In Jesus name I pray Amen.

Dear God

Today is the day that you have made, I will rejoice and be glad about it. In the mist of my heartache, headache and pain I still say thank you, when I look back over my life and all that you have blessed me with I can't complain. Someone's life is much worse than mind, and I'm grateful. Father continue to give strength to those less fortunate than I. Bless the bereaved father, the ones that are trying to come to grips with loosening a love one. Hold us in your loving arms until our tears are less and less. I will bless you Lord at all times, your praise will always be in my mouth, Lord I'm not where I need to be, but I'm better than I was. Thanks for giving me strength to carry on in spite of loosing my mom, my heart is broken but my soul is rejoiceing because I know she's in a better place resting, until we rise again. Forgive me Lord for all of my sins spoken and unspoken. Lord I'm lifting up the name of Pastor Shaw, one of your anointed pastors, bless and heal him in the name of Jesus, I'm lifting up my mother-in law Virgie Copeland, deacon Mosley, my husband Marvin, and all those dealing with sickness touch and heal in the name of Jesus I pray, Amen.

Kathleen Copeland

Dear God

We know that all things work together for the good to them that love you and to them that are called according to his purpose. Thanks for giving your only begotten Son Jesus the Christ to die for our sins that we may have eternal life. Lord thanks for sending grace my way today in the grocery store, you knew I only had a hundred dollars for food and you heard my prayer in line asking not to let the bill be more than what I had, the cashier rang up ninety nine dollars and I knew you had stepped in right on time, thank you Lord, I left smiling, giving thanks to you. To those waiting on a blessing don't give up, my God that I serve is awesome, he's nothing but love, he loves us when we don't love ourselves, He will show up right when you need him. Don't be dismayed, don't get discouraged the Lord will come to your rescue. He will put good people in your life, just ask him, give God a try, you can't go wrong. Lord I'm giving thanks for giving me the ability to write my book of prayers, It's the love I have for you, and wanting to tell others of your goodness. Lord I pray that my book be read all over the states, I want to be able to bless as many people as I can telling them of your goodness and mercy shown to me. I trust you, I love you, I believe in your word, I give you all the honor and the praise. In Jesus name I pray, Amen.

Dear God

I will trust in you with all my heart, and lean not unto thine own understanding. Oh how excellent is thy name in all the Earth. Giving thanks for another day that you have made, you woke me up this morning with the use and activity of my limbs, thanks Lord for the food that I had to eat, thank you for keeping us safe thru the night. Lord it's September 17th. And I'm given thanks for another rainy day every day is a little sweeter than the day before bless those that are hurting those that are lost and cannot find a way out but to take their own life change of mind today Lord let them know that with you all things are possible I pray that those that do not know you and those that do know you will learn that you took there pain and suffering away the day you died on the cross. Lord I give thanks even with the pain in my left hip and the tingling in my fingers because I know you will heal my body at the right time. All of my good days outweigh my bad days and I I'm not going to complain, I'm just going to praise you past my pain. Lord I ask you to bless my neighbors, I'm trying to witness to them about the God I serve, I'll keep on asking them to come worship with me, telling them about a man that loves everybody. I will continue to tell them to delight themselves in you Lord and you will give them the desires of their heart. Psalms 37-4. Lord I'm praying for our young people they are cursing and fighting each other out here in the streets, help me Lord reach at least one of them, They need to know that the wages of sin is death, and if they don't get it right down here they won't get in up there. Lord they need to know that pleasant words are as a honeycomb, sweet to the soul and health to the bones Proverbs 16 24. Bless me to be able to tell them it's not too late, exchange evil for good. I want to tell them that Hell awaits them if they don't change their evil ways. I want to tell them that their soul needs to be anchored in you Lord, When the devil attacks our young people I want to tell them that they need to go in there room, close the door and have a little talk with you Lord, they need to tell you all about their troubles. You didn't bring us this far to leave us, they need to know that you are available morning, noon and night. For every victory in my life I say thank you, even the battles that I lost thank you, for every door that closes in my life thank you for opening up a window. Lord I need to reach our young and old and tell them that nothing is impossible for you. Faith is all we need. Amen.

Dear God

You are my Shepherd I shall not want, it's October and cold out today, giving thanks for another day that you blessed me to see. I went to revival tonight and my soul got happy and I wanted to stay all day. I learned that when a person has been knocked down, did harm, wouldn't follow orders, served time in prison, gets a pardon from the father and the son, who are we to hold on to this man's past. Forgive him for his sin and then bless him. God the father and God the Son forgave a thief hanging next to him on the cross. I love you Lord and I strive to be faithful unto death. Lord as I take this new journey of writing prayers I need you to walk with me, hold my hand Lord when it gets to be a little too much, guide my feet, be a friend when I get a little lonesome Lord, come see about me.

When my enemies, and my foes rise up against me, let them stumble and fall. Lord your truth shall be my shield and buckler, I will show your loving kindness every morning and your faithfulness every night. Lord help me to be mindful of others and their problems. Lord create in me a clean heart and a renewed spirit to live for thee all the days of my life. In Jesus name I pray Amen.

Dear God

You said in your word to be faithful unto death and you will give us a crown of life. I miss my mom so much, when will the pain stop, if I could just hug her one more time, to whisper I love you one more time. Lord I need you to set me free from this pain. I did not come this far to falter, but to be set free. Lord I need to tell mom that she has the key to unlock the door to victory, she shall rise again when the trumpet is blown. You said in your word no "no weapon formed against us shall prosper". Lord I'm giving you all the glory, when I'm knocked down thanks for picking me up and placing my feet on solid ground. Lord with you on my side whom shall I fear, when trouble comes my way I may have to cry sometime, I may have some sleepless nights but it's alright because I know you will fix it for me. Lord I know everyday is not going to be easy, but I pray that you will keep your arms around me. Father God bless my pastor and church family, bless him and his family as he bless the church with words from you. You thought we were worth saving so you stayed on the cross all day Friday and all day Saturday, but early that Sunday morning you got up from the grave with all power in your hands, thank you Lord. Death couldn't hold you., no man could have done what you did, I will shout hallelujah thank you for saving me. Amen.

Dear God

Weeping may endure for a night, but joy comes in the morning. Lord I'm praying for our city, state, government, and nation. We are losing family members to gun violence, terrorism is all around, bombing innocent people, we need you Lord, their are some bad people out to do nothing but harm, keep them from around us, place good people in our circle of life. God you loved us so much that you gave your only begotten Son to die for us and man have made a mess of this world. I know upon your return everything will be made new. Bless us until you come for us. Lord I'm on the battlefield for you, I promise you that I will serve you till I die. Lord for every storm that comes in my life I claim victory, for every mountain you brought me over i give you the praise. There is no unrighteousness in you. Whatever I need I will let my request be known to you. I can do all things through Christ which strengtheneth me. I plead the blood over my family, I speak increase in my finance, I speak good health for me and my family. I speak peace in my home, I speak joy and love in my life, I bless you Lord as you bless my house. I put my trust in you Lord not in man. Lord help me to stay focused on you, let your light shine through me so that every person I meet may feel your presence in my soul. In Jesus name I pray Amen.

Kathleen Copeland

Dear God

I lift my hands up to you, I surrender my life to you, every problem that comes my way, I give to you, I can't fix them on my own, my burdens are too much for me to bear, I need you Lord to take hold of my situations and circumstances and fix them for my good. Cast out fear and remove all doubt that is within me, When I'm falling be there to pick me up, I want to be steadfast, unmoveable always abounding in the work of the Lord. When I can't see a way out I know you can make a way out of no way. I believe at this very moment you are touching hearts, opening doors and lining up the right opportunities in my life. Things may look dark and bleak right now but I have faith that my dawn is coming, you said in your word Lord to wait patiently on you. It's December 15th, I'm in St. Joseph hospital, my blood pressure was too high, thanks for lowering it, I knew you wasn't through with me just yet, I have more work to do. Thanks for my husband being by my side. Guide the doctors hand as you do the healing. Help me to stay calm and trust you to fix whatever is going on with my body. Lord I'm grateful for all that you do for me, I don't take it lightly, every day here on earth I'll say thank you, so many have gone on to take their rest. Wherever you go I will follow you Lord. The devil has no mouth, he can't talk without us, he has no legs he can't walk, it's us that bring him to church, in our homes, our schools. Lord we need to be mindful of our tongue, it's sharp like a two edged sword, some things we say, we can't take back, the damage is already done. Father forgive me for all my sins, In Jesus name I pray Amen.

Dear God

Thanks for giving me unspeakable joy, I'm blessed to be here to see my children and their children grow up. Place a hedge of protection around them each and every day. Thank you Lord for a Christian husband someone I can totally depend on, a man that loves you just as much as I do. I'm grateful for this man he and I lay in bed having bible study every night, excited about reading your word. I pray Lord that my steps will be ordered by you, that I stay encouraged to do good not harm. Lord help those that feel like their mountains are too high to climb so they take there life, let them tell their mountains about our God. Lord I pray that we have kind words in our mouth at all times, we may save a life just for being nice, we don't know what a person may be going through. You said in your word that"you will sustain us and you will never let the righteous be shaken". As I walk by faith guide my footsteps, if I fall pick me up and let me start again. Heavenly Father as I continue to write Katy's book of prayers I pray that something that I write about will help lead them to you. I can see myself standing on the banks of Jordan, waiting for the ships to go sailing by, you took my dad and my brother, you came back and picked up my mom. I depend on you father to light and guide my way through life, to keep my mind stayed on you, so I can be ready when you come for me. My heart is opened to receive your word, let your word come forth and fall down in good soil in my soul. Let your word continue to take root in my life, that I may continue to tell others of your goodness and mercy.

Kathleen Copeland

Dear God

I come boldly unto the throne of grace that I may obtain mercy and find grace to help me in time of need. Lord if you never do anything else for me, you already done enough. Lord thanks for blessing my media day for my book. Lord I see you lining things up in my life, this is why I must study to show myself approved, not been ashamed to tell others of your wonders acts and mighty works. Lord I know what you have for me it is for me. I believe it and receive it with open arms. Lord when the righteous cry out for help thanks for hearing and delivering them from trouble. Thanks for being near the broken-hearted and saving those that are crushed in the spirit. Lord I'm grateful to have you in my life, your word said to come unto me all that labor and are heavy laden and you will give us rest. Heavenly Father thanks for calling us your child, because you know we are like children and needs your help. Thanks for being my rock and my salvation, I fear no one because you are the strength of my life, my entire life rests upon you Lord. My whole being depends on your love for me. Your word is more precious than gold. Thank you for being patient with me as I walk gently through every step of this journey. I love you Lord. In Jesus name I pray Amen.

Dear God

I am grateful for everything you have given me. I'm grateful for my family, my friends, my faith, my love for you and your healing power. Lord it's been a long year since I fell and broke my neck, when I'm in pain I remember what could have happened and I rejoice. Thank you Lord for your powerful touch, I could have been paralyzed, but you said no, with a touch of your finger you worked through the doctor to put me back together again, I will praise you until it's my time to leave this earth. Lord Jesus I am a woman that walks by faith not by sight. I plead the blood of Jesus against any forces of evil that cause me or my family members to speak, act, and think out things that are not in conjunction with your will. 1st Samuel chapter 4 tells us about Eli falling backward and broke his neck and died, because he heard that the sacred chest had been taken by the Philistines. I give thanks that I was spared. God I figured out a long time ago that when I'm going through hard times and I wondered where you were I remembered the Teacher is always quiet during a test. I realize now that once you see that your child can handle the now you will release the next. Thanks for blessing me with the things I need and surprising me with the things that I didn't ask for, you are a awesome God. Today I am claiming my inheritance, there is a miracle out there with my name on it. Lord send your Holy Spirit to direct my pathway. Thank you Lord for giving me the gift, talent, and the abilities to write my book of prayers. Lord you have equipped me with the right words to say and for that I say thank you. In Jesus name I pray Amen.

Dear God

I pray for all those that have been in a storm too long, Let there break through come quickly. I pray that you will work a miracle in our lives, sometimes we may not understand your ways but we must sit still and listen to the Holy Spirit. Lord I pray for my children and grandchildren, put a fence all around them, protect them from all hurt harm and danger. Let them lead a healthy and happy life. Father feed my family with manna from on high. Lord I pray that your word will stay with them if they become lost or confused, put them back on the right tracks to you, let your word never depart from them.

Lord thanks for giving me the gifts, talents, and abilities to enjoy life and accomplish your will. Lord I put my trust in you knowing that you have equipped me for the destiny you have for me. Let me continue to tell others of your goodness and mercy towards me. Keep me clothed in my right mind to serve you forever. Lord I'm giving thanks for your healing touch of my neighbor, you worked a miracle in his life, thank you Lord. He was in a coma state until you woke him up, it's not his appointed time to leave, thank you Jesus. Thanks for covering me with your almighty arms. Lord you are awesome, thanks for going before, beside and behind me. In your word John 14-7you said "peace I leave with you, my peace I give to you not as the world give do I give you."

Dear God

My prayer is that everyone will give their life to you today while they still have time. You said in Hebrew "13ch-5- that you will never fail us or abandon us". All we need to do is believe that you died on the cross for our sins and believe that you are God's son. Because you lived and died we can face tomorrow, all fear is gone, we know who holds our future. Thanks for holding my hand today Lord, Mom's birthday is today and I'm crying tears of sadness, I miss her dearly. Mom's resting in Heaven, I'm here on earth wishing her a happy ninth birthday. Lord please give my family the strength we need to survive the loss of such a great mother, grandmother, great great grandmother, sister, aunt and Friend. The pain is so deep. I will bless you Lord and let your praises continually be in my mouth. I open my heart and hands to you today lord, I release everything that's keeping me from you. Lord search and know my heart, help and show me how to be the person you want me to be. God may your glorious name be lifted up. I cried out to you Lord and you heard my cry, remove the bitterness from my heart and fill the empty space with your love through the power of the Holy Ghost. Lord go back into my memory as I sleep, every hurt that has been done to me, heal that hurt, if I caused hurt to others forgive me., as I say I'm sorry. Father I ask your blessings upon my family and friends, clear away all obstacles that may be in their way. May your hand of protection be upon all of us. Whatever we may be going through guide and protect us. Heavenly father hold us in

Your arms of warmth until we fill protected. Lord those that are lonely and broken hearted may they feel your love for us, let them know that you died for us, and we have time to get right with you. In your word "1st John chapter 4 verse 19 says God is love, we love he because you loved us first". In Jesus name I pray Amen.

THE
OCCASION FOR
GRADUATION

Thanks to all for coming and joining us today as we celebrate the accomplishments, hard work and dedication of our seniors. Thanks to all the parents for being a driving force for our youth. Your dreams have transformed as you've grown and will continue to do so, as you work towards your dream to succeed, regardless if the dream changes creating realistic goals is the first step toward achieving what you want. Graduating from high school is a major accomplishment and your first step toward making your future dreams a reality. Your old life has ended and your new life has just begun. As you make choices in your new walk of life follow your heart, do not let anyone or anything define who you are. What you can achieve in your mind believe it in your heart, with your efforts nothing is impossible regardless of the degree of difficulty. Congratulations graduate, your future looks bright, don't let go of your dream. Always keep them in sight, there is no limitations in what you can achieve. Chase your dreams and always believe in yourself. Do not let anything hinder your quest to be the best, this is your time and your season to soar. As you take the next steps in your life remember you are our hope for tomorrow, you are the bright and shining star, you are blessed and highly favored in all that you do. Let your steps through life be ordered by God. The late and great Maya Angelou said "live your dreams, if one is lucky, a solitary fantasy can totally transform one million realities."

Congratulations this is your final destination on the road to success you have arrived. Father watch over our children in Jesus name I pray Amen.

Dear God

Today I'm crying tears of sorrow, my mom's in heaven, I'm here on earth wishing her a happy nineteenth birthday. I open my heart and hands to you today Lord, I release everything that's keeping me from your best. Search and know my heart Lord, help me and show me how to be the person you want me to be. May your glorious name be lifted up. I cried out to you Lord and you healed me, thanks for removing whatever bitterness that may be in my heart, Lord fill the empty space with love through the power of the Holy Spirit. Go back into my memory as I sleep, every hurt that has ever been done to me, heal that hurt. If I caused hurt to others heal them as well and forgive me. Lord today is Valentine's Day I pray that your blessings be upon my family and friends this day. Clear away all obstacles that may be in there way. May your hand of protection be upon all of us, whatever we may be going through guide us Lord and protect us. Hold us in your arms of warmth until we feel safe. Lord help me to keep trusting in your word, when I'm feeling lonely and weak. Always abounding in your word. I know that the works that I do here on Earth is my reward in Heaven. Lord I do want to hear you say servant well done you have been faithful over a few things, now I will make you ruler over many. In Jesus name I pray, Amen.

Kathleen Copeland

A prayer
for momma

Dear God

Thanks for another day that you have blessed me to see. Lord renew my heart with your strength and purpose for me. Forgive me for my errors of yesterday, let your light shine through me so that others may feel your presence in my soul. Lord take my hand I can't make it without you. Im trying to press on toward the upward way, new heights I'm gaining each and every day but I need you to restore strength to my body, joy and spirit to my soul, my heart is broken, bless my house as we try to bless you. Mom is sleeping in Heaven, she left me to soon, I was baking a cake to celebrate my special day on July 19th 2015, but you called her name before I woke. The moment you left me my heart was split into, one side filled with sorrow and the other side died with you. I can see the undertaker wrapping you in a blanket, my son is holding me tight while I'm screaming I want my mom back, I need you mom, Lord I called out to you to bring her back like you did Lazarus but you didn't answer me, you were saying not now child, your mom needs to rest and sleep until I come back, I hear you saying that your mom was a good servant of the Lord, she was faithful unto death, now I'm giving her a crown of life, I hear you saying daughter you will see your momma again, I prepared a home for her in my father's house, her street is called straight, it's paved with gold, she has 24 Elders in her city, she's not alone. Missing you mom is a heartache that never goes away, I'm trying to live in this world without you, but it will never be the same but the memories will remain the same. Lord please heal my broken heart and my emotional wounds, hold me till I hurt no more. If Heaven had a stairway I would walk up there to bring you home. I miss your presence on today and everyday, you were my rock and my joy you was my everything. Mom I know Heaven is beautiful and for me to see you again I must live a life pleasing to God. Every step I take I'll be taking one for you, every breath I breathe one is for you mom. Heavenly Father I put my hope in you, trusting that you will see me through, believing that faith is the only way Lord bless me as I bless you. Lord God command your Angels to protect me when I feel like I'm falling, when it's too much for me to bear Lord send momma to get me and take me to live with her in her new home that you prepared for her in your father's house. in Jesus name I pray Amen.

Dear God

    I'm giving thanks for another day, I'm asking for total healing for my sister Ann.

    Lord you know her struggles and her pain dealing with the battles of dialysis. Lord she needs a touch from you. Lord her port keeps clogging up, let your hands of deliverance clear that situation up for good. Lord I pray that you give her body the strength it needs to fight the Devil of diabetes. One touch from the masters hand is all she needs. Lord as I sit here calling on you, in your word you said "I shall be healed, save me and I shall be saved."Jeremiah 17-14. Lord I need you to stop by here and see about your child. Give her the energy that she needs to fight. Turn this situation around for good. Heavenly father let her encourage herself to get up out of this hospital, let her know that with you all things are possible, that this is only a test, Joy is coming in the morning. Father God continue to bless my sister life as she bless you, when she's feeling weak, weary, and worn, touch her with your finger of love, carry her in your bosom when she feels like she is falling. Lord let this battle be yours not hers to fight. Let your Angels camp around her door to keep her safe night and day. Lord you are her Jehovah Jireh her provider and seer. Im calling on your holy and righteous name to heal her totally. Your child is sick and I need you to come see about her. The lord is her Shepard and she shall not want, Give her the desires of her heart to be healed and set free from diabetes and dialysis, her financial situations. Let your hands of deliverance clear up her medical problems.

Lord I know you are saying today everything will work out and that you are in control. Heavenly father I know you are aware of her condition and what the doctors are saying, but I need you to come and see about her, she loves you Lord, she honors you. Your word says "in Jeremiah chapter 17-14 says heal me, o Lord, and I shall be healed, save me and I shall be saved, for thou art my praise." Lord I know that with you all things are possible, that you are preparing her body for a miracle. Lord when she's feeling weak, weary and worn come see about her, just one touch from your hands is all she needs. Lord I pray your blessings upon my sister and her family. In Jesus name I pray Amen.

Dear God

I will bless your name past my trials and tribulations. I will never waver with my love towards you. I'm your servant, use me Lord for your good, create in me a right spirit and a mind to want to serve you daily. Heavenly Father bless those that don't believe in your word, those that continue to do harm to others let the devil come out of them so they can experience your love. Lord I'm working on the battlefield for you, I will serve you until I die. Lord help me to continue to be steadfast in my walk with you, I pray that I'll be unmoved, unchanged always abounding in your work. Lord I live to tell others of your goodness and mercy towards me. I want to let the world know that you died on Calvary for them and me, that you saved a thief while you were dieing on the cross, that's nothing but love. When life gets to be too much for me to bear I think of what you went threw that day you hung out there on that cross for our sins. Lord you are awesome, we never would have made it without you. Thank you Jesus for carrying all of our sins. Lord you said in your word Deuteronomy chapter 20 verse 4 "the Lord my God is the one who goes with you to fight for me against my enemies to give me victory." I ask these blessings in Jesus name. Amen.

Dear God

I'm screaming hallelujah thank you Jesus for a loving, kind, caring, wonderful beautiful granddaughter, miss Nyiesha Tenae Cole who graduates from Ross Medical School, April 1st. Lord you know her struggle, you know her story she never wavered. She prayed daily asking you to lead and guide her every step of the way. Been a mom and a full time student was challenging, but she stayed the course, she finished the race, thanks Lord, without you by her side she never would have made it. Lord thanks for covering her, keeping her mind on finishing school and being such a great mom. Lord I ask that you continue to bless her life, let the job she wants be made available to her. Let her remember to give you all the glory, honor and the praise. Heavenly Father you are her Rock and her Salvation, whom shall she fear, Lord you are her light in darkness. Lord when she's feeling overwhelmed lead and guide her in the way that she shall go. Lord bless her with the desires of her heart to be the best Nursing Assistant that she can be. Lord as she takes this new walk in life cover her with your love and blood of protection. Bless my great grandson as his mom makes a future for him. Lord I pray that doors will be opened for her to get the job she wants. Let her footsteps be ordered by you. Thanks for keeping her together when she felt like she was falling apart, you always showed up right on time.

Father God she didn't understand what was happening in her life, but you was lining things up for good, thank you Jesus. Lord I'm grateful that she was raised to love you as a child of God, to give you all the honor the glory in all that she does. Heavenly Father bless her parent and her brother, for being there to help and encourage her to finish school, that she can do all things through Christ which strengthens her. Lord the seed that was planted in her a long time ago, I see it growing, growing and growing. I pray this prayer over my granddaughter life, let her be faithful to you Lord unto death, so that she can wear your crown of life. Amen.

A Prayer For
My Daughter
Lauren M Copeland

Dear God

I'm screaming happy birthday to my beautiful daughter Lauren. Lord thanks for allowing me to be a mom for the third time. Lord it has been a honor and a privilege to help raise such a strong woman who knows how to keep her life in order. For sixteen years I watched her grow and become the kind caring person that she is. From a child she was taught to love and be respectful to others. Lord I pray that you continue to cover her life with your love and blood of protection. When the devil tries to rise up against her, let them stumble and fall. Father God as she begins her new walk in life as a Nurse, I ask that you cover her from the crown of her head to the souls of her feet, whatever challenges come her way let her know that you are already there working it out for her good. Lord thanks for giving her such a kind heart. In your word you said,"Blessed are the pure in heart for they shall see God". Continue to lead and guide her footsteps in the way that she shall go, if her burdens get to be a little too much for her to bear, send Grace and Mercy too see about my child, let her know that you are her provider in times of sickness and trouble, all she has to do is call your name and you will come and see about her, that your line is never busy that you are an on time God. Heavenly Father bless her Dad as he bless you. Thank you Lord for keeping him strong in his faith, never wavering raising his child in a Christian home. Lord I pray that the goals she set for herself that she will be able to accomplish them with you by her side. Bless her circle of friends, keep positive people in her life. Lord I pray this prayer over my child's life, baby girl it's your time and season to soar, fly high, God got you.

Dear God

I thank you for allowing me to rise and see another day that you have given me.

Lord I pray this prayer on behalf of my mother in law, Lord you know her pain, you know her struggle with her hip, Father I pray that you heal her with a touch from the Master's hand. Touch her like you did Peter's mother with a fever, cover her with your love and blood of protection. Let the pain flow from her body, in your word you said In Matthew Chapter 7-"ask and it shall be given". Lord I'm asking in the name of Jesus for total healing if it's your will. Heavenly father you know her faithfulness to you, she is a laborer for you Lord, working daily telling others of your love. Come see about your child Lord, give her the strength to hang in there, to fight pass her pain because joy is coming in the morning. Lord you know her heart, a true servant for the King, bless her from the crown of Her head to the souls of her feet, you are her Jehovah Jireh her provider. Lord let the pain that she is experiencing right now be a test of the greatness you have in store for her.

Lord I pray that Mom continue to be steadfast unchangeable abounding in your work in spite of her pain, let her know Lord that this pain she's feeling is only temporary. In Jeremiah chapter17-14 you said" heal me, o Lord, and I shall be healed, save me, and I shall be saved for thou art my praise." Lord you are moms

Shepard she shall not want, I pray that you give her the desires of her heart to be healed and set free from pain. Bless her family as they bless you. I pray this prayer of healing over my mother in law's health. In Jesus name I pray, Amen.

Dear God

I'm giving thanks to you today for blessing me with an amazing Sister, Debbie, Lucas. Lord the day she was born we knew she was a great gift from you to our family.

Lord you blessed her with the natural gift to discern your holy and righteous word, thank you Lord. You blessed her with a kind loving spirit, telling others of your love and goodness whereever she goes. Heavenly Father we are so honored and blessed to have your child in our mist. Lord when she was sick you stepped in right on time to come see about your child. Lord i can hear you saying daughter, watch me work my miracle on you so others will believe that I am the true and living God. Lord she kept the faith, she never wavered away from your word, thank you Jesus, for being such a awesome God. Heavenly Father down through the years she has been filled with the precious gift of the Holy Ghost, ministering to the sick, caring for others, and keeping her house blessed with your word. Lord my sister raised her only Son to love and respect your word, to teach his three children about the love of Christ. Thank you for blessing her with a wonderful husband who has been by her side since high school, Lord you blessed her marriage to the love of her life Robert Lucas. I give thanks for a wonderful brother-In-law who takes care of his family and home. Heavenly Father I pray that you shower down blessings from on high for my sister and her family. Lord keep her in good health, let her continue to minister to those that don't know you in the pardon of their sins. Lord I pray this prayer over the life of my sister, my friend, In Jesus name I pray Amen.

Dear God

I'm screaming happy Birthday to my sister my best friend Joyce Maschat. Heavenly Father thank you for blessing me with an amazing friend for fifty six years who has stuck by me during the good times and the bad. Lord you put people in our lives for a reason, and some for only a season. Lord the friendship we share is unconditional it is priceless, for that I say thank you. Lord you blessed me with a caring and loving friend, that I don't have to talk to everyday, but when we need each other we are there. Lord I pray that you bless her family, keep your arms of protection all around them. Keep her in good health and strength. Lord bless her children and their children.

Lord bless her house as she bless you, I pray that you keep her in perfect peace, give her the desires of her heart. Heavenly Father continue to be her Jehovah Jireh, her provider all the days of her life. Enlarge her territory. When she's feeling weak, weary, and torn, Lord I pray that you step in right on time, let her know that there's nothing to hard that you can't solve. Continue to be her Rock and her Salvation, her light in darkness, her hope for tomorrow. Lord if her enemies or that one called the Devil shall rise up against her, I pray that they shall stumble and fall. Lord I pray this prayer over my friend life that you will open up a window and pour her out a blessing that will be too much for her to receive.

Dear God

Today is March 13th I'm giving thanks for another day of life that you have given me. Heavenly Father be Lord of my life today, take control of my heart, keep me

From sinning against you today Lord. I pray for wisdom and knowledge of your Word.

Lord use my life today to glorify your name. Father create in me a clean heart and a new and right spirit within me. Lord I pray for peace when chaos is all around me. Lord I want my record to be there at the Judgement Bar, in that great gettin up morning. Lord guide my way because I can't make it without you. Shine through me Lord so that every person I meet or see may feel your presence in their souls. Lord I pray for perfect peace within my family. Continue to bless our home and family, strengthen my husband as he takes care of our home. Lord I will not forget all of your benefits you blessed me with. Lord I won't forget that you healed all of our diseases and crowned us with your loving kindness and tender mercies. Heavenly Father no matter what I'm going through or facing I'll remember that no weapon formed against me shall prosper, I walk by Faith not by sight in all that I do. In Jesus name I pray Amen.

Dear God

Thanks for creating the heavens and the earth, and everything that is in it. Adam and Eve caused sin to appear in the world but you blessed us anyway, thank you Lord. Lord I pray that you bless us as we strive to live Holy, to do what is acceptable your perfect will. Lord continue to bless the sick and those that are confined to their homes. Heavenly Father oh what a privilege it is to carry all our burdens to you in prayer.

Lord thanks for all that is good in my life. I'm standing on the promises that you made to us Lord. To live for you all the days of my life so that I will able to live again in your home.

Even though we were born into sin, we was shaped by your word to live a Godly life. Lord I pray that you bless my household, keep us grounded and our minds stayed on you. Lord continue to fight my battles as I try to keep my mind stayed on you, Lord the emptiness that I'm feeling from the lost of my Mom I pray that you replace it with your love. Lord I'm praying for those that know you, but is not trying to come and worship with you. Lord give me an encouraging word that I can say to them kindly that they need to come and listen to the Shepherd as he feeds the Church. Lord I want to tell others that some day they will need to call on you and you may not answer. Lord I know the scripture says absent from the body, present with the Lord, but I'm feeling weak, weary and torn, I'm missing my mom so much, Lord when will the hurt stop. I can hear mom saying daughter "I'm at peace in my Father's

Kathleen Copeland

house, he's feeding me with manna from on high so stop worrying about me and live, God hears your cry and he will come and comfort you. My room has been prepared for me in my Father's house, there's nothing up here but peace and happiness. Daughter you have to live to see me again, my day on Earth was up, rejoice and be glad for me, I will see you again. In Jesus name I pray Amen.

Dear God

Today is the day that you have made and I will rejoice and be glad about it.

Lord in spite of my heartache, headache and pain I will say thank you. When I look back over my life and all that you have blessed me with I can't complain. Someone else is much worse than I am. Lord strengthen those less fortunate than I, Bless those that are going through bereavement like I am. Lord hold us in your arms until the tears are less and less. Lord I'm not where I need to be but I'm better than I was. Lord forgive me for my sins spoken and unspoken. Father God bless Pastor Shaw, continue to give him and sister Shaw strength to go on. Lord thank you for sending grace my way today knowing I only had a hundred dollars the cashier rang up ninety nine, thank you Lord you are an on time God. Lord my book is selling, it's the love I have for you and the desire to tell others of your goodness that's keeping me going. Lord i want to reach as many people as I can, telling them that you died on the cross for everyone. Lord you have been better to me than I have been to myself, thank you Jesus. Lord, bless our young people, they are killing each other everyday. I want to reach out to them and tell them that the wages of sin is death. Lord I want to tell them that pleasant words are as a honeycomb sweet to the soul, and health to the bones. Lord I want to be able to tell others it's not too late to exchange evil for good. Lord I know my soul is anchored in you, even when I don't feel like going on, it's something about that name Jesus that brings me back and lets me know that you have done enough. Lord I know in my heart for me to get near the cross I can't stop praising your name. Lord I know you didn't bring me this far to leave me. Thanks for being available to me morning, noon, and night.

Thank you Lord for every victory in my life, even the battles that I lost. For every door that was closed in my life, thank you Lord for opening up a window and pouring me out a blessing that was too much for me to receive. These blessings I ask in Jesus name Amen.

Dear God

As I take this new journey of writing prayers I need you to walk with me. Lord hold my hand when it gets to be a little too much, guide my feet, be a friend when I get a little lonesome. Lord when my enemies and my foes rise up against me let them stumble and fall. Lord I pray that you let your truth be my shield and buckler. Heavenly Father you called one of your faithful servants home today. Deacon Mosley was a true laborer and a kind, caring, loving friend and neighbor. Lord bless his family as they go through these difficult days ahead. He fought a good fight, he finished the race, he's waiting for his Crown of life. Good night our friend, we will look for you in your new home on straight street, where the street is paved with gold, in your father's house that he has prepared for you. Even in death Lord let us continue to be strong, telling others that will come in the morning. Trust you with our heart because you won't put more on us than we can bear. In Jesus name I pray Amen.

Heavenly Father

It's thursday March 31 st 2016, I'm thanking you for sending your Angels to camp around my door last night. Thanks for keeping the thieves and robbers away. Thanks for your touch Lord, you kept me pain free through the night and then you woke me up early this morning with my mind stayed on you. Lord thanks for lifting me up today, when no b or nothing could help me your love is what keeps me and sustains me. I can hear you saying, daughter it's alright to ask me to bless and heal you, you are my child, as you pray for others, pray for yourself as well, I am your provider in sickness, in good health, even in death, call on me I will hear and come to see about you. Lord i will forever give you the honor and the glory in all that I do. You are my Rock, my Sword, my Shield, my strength at all times. Lord you made me unique from birth. You put all of my organs on the opposite side of everyone else. My heart as well as all the other organs are opposite, doctors call it complete sites inversus, I call it love. You was setting me apart from others, thanks Lord. The gift of prayer is what you gave me. Lord I will love you unto death. In Jesus name I pray Amen.

Heavenly Father

I come before you with a bowed down head and a humble heart giving thanks for blessing Second Baptist Church with Pastor George Waddles Jr. and first Lady Angela Waddles and family for the past two years. Heavenly Father you placed an anointed man of God to feed your church with manna from on high, and I say thank you Lord. The two years that Pastor has been here with us the membership has grown tremendously. Souls have been saved and faith in you Lord has been restored. Lord I pray that you continue to bless Pastor as he bless you. Father God thanks for blessing SBC with a kind and caring First Lady, She exemplifies all the qualities of a loving and understanding Pastor's wife, let her light continue to shine within her so that others can see her good works. Lord bless their children, cover them with your love and blood of protection, let their steps be ordered by you in all that they do. Father God bless Pastor with good health and strength, when he's feeling weak, weary and torn, send Grace and Mercy to see about him. Lord let him stand on the promises of Christ our Savior, to let go and let you handle the storms and trials that may come before him. Lord I pray that you bless Pastor's parents and siblings, let the love continue to flow from Michigan to Chicago. I pray that the love Pastor Waddles have for Second will be as the love Jesus had for everyone that loved him. Lord I pray this prayer over the life of Pastor and Sister Waddles life, I pray that you open up a window and pour them out a blessing that's too much for them to receive. Let the duties of being a Pastor continue to line up with your orders of being Pastor of the Second Baptist Church of Ypsilanti, Michigan. Lord I pray that Pastor continues to show Charity out of a pure heart and of a good conscience for members here at SBC, thanks you Lord for sending us a wise and knowledgeable man to lead us, In Jesus name I pray Amen.

Dear Heavenly Father

I'm giving thanks for another day that you have given me on Earth.

Lord I'm feeling sick with a cold but I'm going to praise you anyway. Lord you been so good to me, I just want to say thank you. Sometimes we have to encourage ourselves, to speak life over ourselves. Im deeply loved, profoundly cherished and equipped in your word. Lord nothing or no one can keep me from your highest and best will for me. Lord I will follow you and your will for me, I will try to accomplish the impossible and love the unloveable that come into my life, Lord I am your living testimony because Jesus lives inside me. I'm alive today because you kept me, someone prayed for me, thank you Lord for your Grace and Mercy towards me. Lord I believe you created me for a special purpose and I know that you have a special plan for my life, Lord please fulfill your purpose for me, and help me do all that I can to earnestly seek you in prayer and the hearing of your word. Continue to guide my footsteps as I walk in the newness of Christ.

In Jesus name I pray Amen.

Kathleen Copeland

Heavenly Father

I bless your Holy and Righteous name. I bow before you to ask you to heal my son's broken heart. Lord let his child stay safe in your arms. Protect her from all hurt harm and danger. Lord we may not understand your plan but I know you will reveal it to us soon. Let my son close his eyes, take a deep breath and say," God, I know it's your plan, just help me through it, when all I have is you, then all I need is all I have. Lord you know everything about me and I pray constantly to you to keep me saved, filled with the precious gift of the Holy Ghost. Lord I know you can make the very worst things that ever happened in our lives work for your very best. I praise your name and I claim victory over my enemies, I speak life over my children and their children, in Jesus name I pray. Amen.

Heavenly Father

I'm giving thanks for another day that you have blessed me to see. Father I'm praying today for a special young man. Lord this young man took a life when he was young and foolish. Now he is a man and realizes his mistakes, Lord my prayer is that he will come to you and ask for forgiveness for the wrong that he did. Lord I know his heart is heavy and if he had a second chance he would make the right choice. Lord I pray that you will forgive him so that he can forgive himself and ask the victim's family for forgiveness. Lord I'm praying for him and with him. I'm thankful for my struggles because without it, I wouldn't have stumbled across my strength. Lord grant Michael the serenity to accept the things that he cannot change, give him the courage to change the things that he can with you by his side. Let him accept hardship as a pathway to peace. Lord I pray that Michael will make all things new by surrendering to your will and your ways. Keep your arms of protection all around him each and every day of his life. Lord help him to remember that our purpose here on Earth is not to get lost in the dark, but to be a light to others, so that they may find their way through us. Lord just like you used Saul for your good, use michael. He is your son that has fallen, but have gotten back up. Lord if it's your will, I pray that he be given a second chance to live, to love, to follow after right in all that he does. Heavenly Father I pray this prayer over Michael's life. In Jesus name I pray Amen.

Heavenly Father

I come before you with pain all over my body. Lord I ask for total healing in the mighty name of Jesus. Lord it's Good Friday and I'm been admitted into the Hospital. I pray that you work through the Doctors to find the source of my pain. Lord let there be no cancer or any other sickness growing inside my body, if it is please remove it. Bless all the sick here at St. Joseph Mercy Hospital. Give them the strength to hold on and wait on you to heal them if it's your will. Bless my husband as he sits by my side. Lord I praise you and give you all the honor and the glory in the mighty name of Jesus. Had it not been for your grace and mercy I never would have made it. Lord I'm not going to complain just asking you for total healing. Lord I'm giving thanks for my Pastor coming to have prayer with my husband and myself. Continue to bless him as he bless us. Lord place your hedge of protection all around us each and every day. I pray this prayer over my health, In Jesus name Amen.

Heavenly Father

Thanks for another day's journey that you brought me through. Today most people are celebrating their Mothers, I'm sitting here crying because mine is not here, Instead I should be celebrating that she is with you and that's the best Mother's Day anyone should want, knowing their loved one is resting in Heaven not down here in this place called Earth. Lord I pray for strength for my family, we are struggling trying to tiptoe around our feelings. Bless others that may be going through the same changes. A Mothers love is irreplaceable. Once she's gone you can't get another one. Thank you Lord for allowing my Mom to see all of her children grow into mature adults. To be able to see all of her grandchildren and greatgrands. Mom departed this life July 19th 2015, but the pain feels like today. I miss her more and more each day, I just need to talk to her, to see her smile that beautiful smile she had. Mom you too are a winner. Sleep on Mom, I will get it together soon, watch over your children till we see you again. In Jesus name I pray Amen.

Heavenly Father,

Thank you for this day that you allowed me to see. Thanks for being able to see, hear, touch, feel and walk this morning. Lord thanks for providing a way for those less fortunate than I. Lord i'm blessed because you are a forgiving God, who understands and knows my needs, for that I say thank you. Forgive me for sins known and unknown. Continue to keep us safe from harm seen and unseen dangers. I give you all the honor and the glory. Lord I love you, and I need you, come into my heart and bless me, my family, my home and my friends. Heavenly Father I know these difficult times I face are not meant to shatter my life or my faith but to make my faith stronger, thanks for always being there to pick me up when I fall. Lord you are my refuge in times of need, my strength and joy.

Heavenly Father

I give thanks for another day that you have blessed me to see. I'm praying this prayer for my Sister and Brother in Christ, James and Patricia Chandler.

Lord continue to bless them with your love and keep your arm's of protection around them and their son's. Lord continue to be there Jehovah Jireh in all that they do. When their hearts are heavy, weary, weak and torn please step in to guide them in the right direction that they should follow. Lord my prayer is that the Chandlers will be steadfast unchangeable, always abiding in your word, no matter what challenges come their way.

I pray that their steps will be ordered by you. Father bless their Son's, you know their story, when a mother's heart is broken only you can mend it. Lord you are a God of second chances, I'm praying that you put this family back together again. Heavenly Father send Grace and Mercy to see about your children. If it is your will, I pray that you will give them the desires of their hearts. Continue to bless them as they bless you. I pray this sprayer over the lives of my Sister and Brother in Christ. In Jesus name I pray Amen.

Heavenly Father

Thanks for another day that you allowed me to see. Thanks for my health and strength. Lord thanks for taking my family to Hawaii safe, and bringing us home safe. Your Grace and Mercy was with us, for that I say thank you. Lord please continue to bless my family, comfort the bereaved, give them the strength to make it from one day to the next. Lord you know we lost our great nephew, bless the parents, grands and siblings of baby Dionte. I pray that they seek you and change their life for good. Father bless those that are lost and have no hope in seeking you, I pray that they turn from their ways that's not pleasing in your sight. Lord I pray that I stay in your grace, seeking to learn of you and follow after Christ. Forgive me for all of my sins, create in me a clean heart and a new zeal to live for you all the day's of my life. Continue to bless my husband and the love that we share for each other. Father cover my children and grands, keep them safe from hurt and danger, bless their life, and let them have life more abundantly. Watch over my sisters and brothers, and their families. Bless our finances Lord, where we are lacking, I pray for increase. Bless those that don't know where their next Penney will come from. Supply all of our needs. Lord continue to bless those that are fighting for our lives in the military, bless the President of our United States, and his family. Father God bless our Pastor and our church family. Give Pastor manna from on high, to preach the Gospel to his congregation. Lord continue to bless my life, when I seem to be falling, Lord pick me up and put me back together again. I pray this prayer in Jesus name Amen.

Heavenly Father

My heart is heavy today, knowing that you woke me up this morning, protected my family as we slept last night, you have been better to me than I have been to myself. I long for my mom, I miss her so much, my heart aches for her, I know where she is, and I know I should handle it better, but I'm stuck, I can't get to the next step. If she was here today we would be in Tuscaloosa Alabama at the family reunion. But instead I was sent a place setting in her honor. Lord I know people are losing their parents every day, some children, but it's so hard to let it go, my grieving may last forever. I know some people think you grieve for awhile, and you let it go, I can't. When I can't sleep I wrap my mom's throw around me. I can still smell her scent on it. The Word says weeping may endure for a night, Joy cometh in the morning, I need my morning, right now. Help me Lord, heal this broken heart. Let me never forget the memories mom and I made together. Bless all the bereaved, comfort them as well. I pray this prayer over my life, in Jesus name, Amen.

Heavenly Father

Thank you for giving me a loving, kind, caring husband of ten years. You blessed me with a wonderful man of God. Let the love we share continue to flow through us. Bless my marriage Lord, let us continue to put you first in all that we do. Let the love we share carry us through the good as well as the bad days here on Earth. Let us love each other beyond our pain, knowing that you will always be there for us. Cover us with your love and blood of protection. Hold us in your arms when we feel like we are falling. Lord, give us many years together here on Earth. July 3 2006 what you put together, let no man try to separate the love that Marvin and I have for each other. In Jesus name I pray, Amen.

Heavenly Father

Thanks for giving me another day here on Earth to worship you. Lord you know Our hearts are heavy once again. My nephew lost his three year old, who was hit by a car. Lord bless that family, bring them some closure. Give them strength to handle the loss. Bless all the families that was affected by this great tragedy. It's July 9th and it's only been two weeks since another nephew has buried his grand baby. The nephews losing their grandchildren so early really hurts. Lord we know you don't make mistakes, just help us to understand it by and by. Father the world is so messed up right now, the Police that took a oath to protect us, is killing us, one Black person at a time, and nothing is being done. We come together and pray, and say black lives matter until another one is killed. Lord I know you see the shape we are in, and I know it hurts to see what you created is being destroyed by man, I pray that we come together and fixed this mess before it's too late. Forgive us Father, for all the sins that we have committed. Help us live together here on Earth before we miss our chance to live with you in Heaven. These and all blessings I ask in Jesus name. Amen.

Kathleen Copeland

Heavenly Father

Thank you for keeping me safe and in my right mind, Lord I am so grateful for your kindness and mercy shown towards me. I have seen some good days and I have experienced some bad ones as well, but through it all I'm not going to complain. If I never receive another blessing you have blessed me enough. When I didn't do right you still kept me, when I felt like I was going to lose my mind you put your arms of protection around me and kept me close. Lord all I can say is thank you. When I went left instead of right you were there to guide my footsteps, and to point me in the right direction. Lord I have made a lot of mistakes in my past that I can't undo and I know I shouldn't reflect on the things that you have placed in the sea of forgiveness, never to bring up again, but I won't ever forget how you changed me, my past is just that, my past my future is you. Trying to get my name written in the lamb's book of life, Lord I surrender my all to you, no other help I know if thou withdraw thyself from me where shall I go. I love you Lord and I will lift my voice wherever I go to worship you, to always give you the praise. Thank you Lord for giving your only begotten Son to die that we may have life and have it more abundantly. Heavenly Father I ask that you cleanse me and make me whole forever and ever more. In Jesus name I pray Amen.

Heavenly Father

As I prepare for bed tonight keep me safe in our home, keep death, sickness, thieves and robbers away. Bless us with great dreams calmness and peace as we sleep. Lord wake us in our right mind on the morning, give us the use and activities of our limbs. Wake us up to see another new day that you have given us. Lord bless us as we travel up and down the highways today, Father let me be a blessing to others on today, telling someone about your goodness and mercy towards me. Lord let something that I may say lead someone to you. In your word you said, "if I be lifted up from this earth I'll draw all men unto me." Let someone come crying saying what must I do to be saved. Lord I give thanks for my life, I'm not perfect, I make mistakes, I fall, but with your help I get back up. Lord I pray that you continue to bless my life, let me continue to write my prayers to you, so that others may read and want to get to know the God I serve. Lord give me wisdom and understanding of your word. Lord bless those that are dealing with sickness in their bodies, heal them Lord, with a touch of your hand. Bless my mother In law, heal her body from all aches and pain. Bless our friends and their sickness, heal in the mighty name of Jesus. I pray for our children that are going off to college, put your arms of protection around them each and every day. Lord I pray for us that are struggling with our finances, bless us with our needs. You know our wants and you know what we desire, bless us according to our needs. Let us continue to work for our wants. Keep us in your care Lord all the days of our lives, in Jesus name I pray Amen.

Kathleen Copeland

Dear God

It's August 16, 2016 I ask that your will be done in my life today. Lord with you on my side I know that I can do all things through Christ who strengthens me. What you have for me to do today Lord I'm willing. I want to serve you and only you. Lord when I'm feeling low and down I want to call mom but instead I call you, my Lord of Lords and King of Kings. Help me make it through, times of weariness and pain, give me strength to make it through another day. A life without a Mother to call on is hard, but with you all things are possible. Lord bless those that are standing in the need. Some are worse than most of us, give them the desires of their hearts, if it's your will. Lord continue to watch over my brothers and sisters, helping us to stay close and love each other as our Mother would want. Bless my husband as he blesses you, give him good health and strength to continue on his journey of learning of your goodness and mercy. Bless his walk with you Lord, supply his needs. In Jesus name I pray Amen.

Heavenly Father

Today you blessed me and my family to see my son get married. He is marrying the love of his life Shon Smith, Lord I pray that you bless them and their marriage. Let nothing or no one separate them from the love of each other and you. Bless their children, let them show nothing but love towards each other. Heavenly Father it's September 3rd and I'm grateful to be alive to witness such a grand occasion, wishing Mom was here to see her grandson be married. Lord help me to remember to always pray for our children, please keep your love and blood of protection over them. Bless them as they bless you. Lord I bow before you to give thanks for all you have done for me, treating me better than I have been to myself. Lord thanks for picking me up each and every time I was falling. Forgive me for all of my sins. Lord you know the devil is busy, right when things are doing good he walks in and mess things up, give me the strength to defeat this devil. Bless me to stay in control of my life, making it about you, not me or mine. Lord I pray to put others before me in all that I do. Help me to show loving kindness at all times. Continue to bless my family, give them good health and strength. Bless those that are worse off than we are. In Jesus name I pray Amen.

Kathleen Copeland

Dear God

Thanks for another day of life. Thanks for early morning rising in my right mind. Lord you had your Angels watch over us all day and night and I say thank you. Lord thanks for being our Shepherd and letting me be on your wake up list this morning. Lord from the bottom of my heart I want to thank you for being with me all the way for never leaving me for always loving me in spite of my faults. Whoever shall call on your name shall be heard and saved. Thanks for this personal relationship that I have with you Lord. You are truly the center of my joy. I can come to you with all my cares and concerns and know you will hear and answer in your own time. The word say's count it all joy, my brothers, when you meet trials of various kinds, for you know that the testing of your faith produces steadfastness. And let steadfastness have its full effect, that you may be perfect and complete, lacking in nothing. James- ch-1-2-4. Lord help me to stay focused on you and to never give up on myself, especially when things are not not lining up the way I think they should be. Lord step in and guide me the way that you will have me go. Give me patience to be still and to wait on a word from you. In all that I do, I will give you the honor and the glory. I pray this prayer in Jesus name Amen.

Cancer

Dear God,

My prayer is for those suffering from Cancer, I ask in Jesus name for total healing, restore bodies that have been affected by cancer, if it's your will. Lord I ask you to restore faith that has been shattered by the news. Let them know that you don't make mistakes, that everything that happens to us is not always your will, but sometimes the Devils. Lord I reckon that the sufferings of this present time are not worthy to be compared with the glory which shall be revealed in U. S. Romans ch-8-18. KJV. Lord I know there will be times when we don't understand the why, when, or where that happens in our life, that's when we learn to fully trust you no matter what comes our way. Lord help us to have that unwavering faith that will get us through. Bless those fighting, to hang in there, and trust you. You are the God on the mountain and in the valley. Let those battling cancer know that you are arranging things in your favor and making a way even when they don't see a way. Lord you created us, and when the body is sick heal us. Lord repair the body that you made for us, refresh our soul you created for eternal existence, you alone know how to restore our health, for you made us. Lord make us whole again so that we may live our life for you. Amen.

Today Heavenly Father

I'm giving thanks for another day of life that you have given me. Lord I'm praying for all the children that are waiting to be adopted, Lord let someone's heart be touched today and say yes to a child, let them opened up their home to love and care for a child that needs a home, regardless of their age. Let love flow from the baby's to the youth. Bless the parents that had to give them up for whatever reason. Lord we know that children are a blessing no matter how they got here. Lord those that take our children into their homes I pray that they treat them well. Cover them with your love and blood of protection. To the children, don't give up, have faith, believe, for I am your God, I will strengthen and help you, I will uphold you with my righteous right hand. So do not fear I am with you. Isaiah 41-10 -NIV-. Lord you said in your word suffer little children to come unto me, and forbid them not, for of such is the kingdom of God, Luke ch-18-16.

Lord, children are the future, help us to keep them safe, healthy, and happy. In Jesus name I pray Amen.

Heavenly Father

My heart is so heavy today, our people are being killed daily by the police and each other. The signs are here that you are coming and coming soon. Lord I am making ready for your return, getting my heart fixed and my mind stayed on you. Help me to continue to create in me a clean heart and a right spirit to serve you daily. Lord I want to be alive to see you coming in the clouds, to look upon your face, to be caught up in the air to meet your arrival. Lord I pray that I will be taken to live with you in heaven, never to see death, sickness, sorrow, pain, hunger, killings any more. To live in peace with you forever and ever. Lord I pray that you continue to bless my family's life, let us continue to serve you no matter how bad the world is, to stay focused on you and living the best life that we can while we still have time. Cover our children, keep the devil away from them, shower them with your love and blood of protection. Bless our enemies, those that wish to harm us, bless them as well. Lord in your word Micah chapter 6 you showed us that you stand for righteousness and justice. I pray that others will listen and adhere to your word. My prayers are for those hurting each other to realize that they are hurting you, who died for us, that we may have life and have it more abundantly. Lord no matter what the future holds, I will hold to your unchanging hand, to be steadfast, unmoveable always abounding in your work. I may not know what the future holds for me, but I do know who holds my future. I love you Lord with all my heart, mind and soul. I pray this prayer over my life, and the life of my love ones, in Jesus name I pray Amen.

Dear God,

    As I start my day today thank you for life, forgive me for all of my sins, help me to start my day fresh with a renewed heart and mind. Lord thank you for watching over me and my love ones all night long. Lord I know I can do all things through you that gives me strength, Philippians chapter 4:13. Lord if someone is hurting today kindly embrace them, comfort them and make them whole, if it's your will. Lord I'm waiting patiently on you, incline me and hear my cry. Lord you brought me up also out of a horrible pit, out of the miry clay, and you set my feet upon a rock that you established for my goings. Lord thank you for putting a new song in my mouth, many shall see it and fear, some shall trust in you. In Jesus name I pray Amen.

Dear God,

Giving thanks to my Wonderful Counselor, The Mighty God, The Everlasting Father, The Prince of Peace-Isaiah chapter 9:6 for another day that you have blessed me to see. Lord I trust in you and will find strength in you. Heavenly Father I want to soar high on wings like a Eagle, help me Lord to run and not grow weary, I want to walk and not faint if it's your will, Isaiah 40:31. I'm blessed, I'm happy, I'm saved and I'm grateful for all you have done for me. If a door shuts on me, I will keep banging until you open up a window and pour me out a blessing that may be too much for me to bear. Lord thank you for loving me so much that you gave up your life so that I may live. You are truly my King of Kings and Lord of Lords. Jesus you are my hope for tomorrow, my joy in time of sorrow, my wheel in the middle of a wheel, you are my all and all. Thank you Lord for your constant presence in my life. You are always with me, even when I feel like I'm all alone, you are never absent, always near, Deuteronomy chapter 31:6. Thank you for walking with me, being by my side each and every day. Lord you said in your word "to come, to you all who are weary and burdened, and I will give you rest."Matthew chapter 11:28. Thank you for the rest, joy and peace that you have given me. In Jesus name I pray Amen.

A Prayer for My Brother In Law-Charles Copeland

Dear God,

Today I'm giving thanks to you for blessings me with an amazing brother in law. Lord we are blessed twice when we are given a wonderful Brother, and now a great Brother in law. Lord I pray that you cover him with your love and blood of protection. My Prayer is that you keep him safe and in good health and strength. Heavenly Father if it's Your will I pray that you will let knowledge of you fall fresh on Charles, open his mind and heart to receive you. Let him know that you love him so much that you died on the cross for him, so that he to shall live again. Lord my prayer is that you bless Charles with good health and strength. Lord when he's feeling weak, weary, or torn, lift him up. Place the desire in his heart to call upon your Holy and Righteous Name, to believe that you will come and see about your child. Bless his family and love ones. Lord I pray that you hold Charles close in the palm of your hand. Continue to bless his Mother, Sisters and Brothers as they bless you. Place the desire in Charles heart to continue to Honor his Mother so that his days may continue to be long upon this Earth. I pray this prayer over the life of my brother in law Charles Copeland, In Jesus name I pray Amen.

A Prayer For
My Cousins George
And Gwen Wilson

Dear God,

    I'm praying over the life of two of my Cousins George and Gwen Wilson. Lord thank you for blessing our family with two of the kindness, caringness people on this Earth. Lord thank you for placing them in our family and circle of friends that truly love you. Heavenly Father I pray that you cover them with your love and blood of protection. Bless their family and continue to lead them in your path of righteousness for your namesake. Lord bless them with good health and strength, where their bodies are torn down please restore their health. Take away the pain that have entered their bodies, make them whole again. Lord you said in your word, Mark chapter 11:24 "therefore I say unto you, what things soever ye desire, when ye pray, believe that ye receive them, and ye shall have them." Lord I'm believing and trusting that you will give them a long life that's pleasing in your site, without hurt and pain. Father bless them as they bless you, if it's your will. Continue to bless their child and grandchildren, I pray that they walk in the footsteps of their parents. To love others and become great servants of the most high. Let them show forth their loving kindness as their parents did. Lord thank you for allowing me to see and witness the light that shines inside George and Gwen, they are true examples of what a servant of the Lord should be like. I pray that when it's your time to call and their time to answer that my Cousins will be caught up in the air too meet you upon your return. In Jesus name I pray Amen

A Prayer For
My Brother- David
Earl Clifton

Heavenly Father

I'm giving thanks today October 24th 2016, for blessing me with an amazing, kind, caring, and joyful individual that I call Brother, but in reality he's my warrior, my protector, my peacemaker, and the love of my life, my little big brother David Earl Clifton. Lord thank you for blessing our family with such a loving young man who will and knows how to take charge and care for his family. Lord as I watched him grow, I knew he was destined to be a great leader, a wonderful husband, and an amazing father and grandfather. Lord thank you for blessing my brother with a wonderful wife that loves him unconditionally. Thanks for putting good people in his circle of friends, never leading him astray. Lord continue to cover him and his family with your love and blood of protection, keep your arms around him day and night. Lord you have given him the desires of his heart to walk as your servant, to always give you the honor and the glory in all that he does for that I say thank you. Bless him and his family as they bless you. My prayer is that David continues to serve and honor you in all that he does so that when it's your time to call us and I'll time to answer we will be caught up in the air to meet you, our parents and brother. In the mighty name of Jesus I pray this prayer over the life of my brother and his family in Jesus name Amen.

A Birthday Prayer For My Daughter-Marquita Latreace Slater

Heavenly Father

I'm giving thanks today October 25, 2016 for blessing me with an amazing, kind, caring, loving individual that I call my baby, my rock, my strong tower, my beautiful daughter. Thank you for allowing me to be a Mother to such a strong wonderful young woman that brings me nothing but joy. Lord I give thanks for letting me teach her about you and your love for the world, that you died for us all. Lord continue to bless her and protect her and her children and grandchildren. My prayer is that her walk with you will be continuously. To always acknowledge you and let you direct her pathway. Lord bless my daughter to have good health and strength, to be the strong woman that she is. When she's feeling weak weary or torn carry her until she can stand again. Lord open up a window and pour her out a blessing that is overflowing for her and her family. Continue to bless her as she cares and protects her children and grandson. Cover them day and night with your love and blood of protection. Lord I pray that my daughter's light shines within wherever life takes her. I pray this prayer over the life of my child and her children, in Jesus name I pray, happy birthday baby girl know that you are a special gift from God and loved so much, continue to smile and watch God's Blessings. You are so deserving and hardworking. Love you to the Moon and back.

A Birthday Prayer For My Friend – Mr. William (Bill) Johnson

Heavenly Father

Today September 20th 2016, I give thanks for blessing me to know an amazing upright man of God whom I call my friend, Mr. William Johnson. Lord I give thanks for my friend Geri for having such a loving, kind and caring husband that loves her unconditionally. Lord thank you for blessing their marriage and their family with your Love and protection. Father thanks for allowing my friend to celebrate another year that you have blessed him to see. Keep him in good health and strength to see many more wonderful years. Lord I feel honored to be in their circle of friends, to be blessed to see what true friendship really means. Lord you have placed good people in my life and I am truly grateful, continue to be their Jehovah Jirah, their provider for all of their needs. Bless them Father as they bless you. Heavenly Father I pray that you bless there son and his family, hold them in the palm of your hands. Lord I give thanks for William and Geri for been a true Servant of the King, knowing and telling others of your goodness and mercy towards them and others. Father I pray that the friendship that we share be a long one, that we will be friends in our new home that you have prepared for us. Father in your word you said, "A man that hath friends must shew himself friendly, and their is a friend that sticketh closer than a brother, thank you Lord for allowing William and Geri to be those friends. I pray this prayer over the life of my dear friend William and his family, Lord bless him to see many more wonderful Birthdays, in Jesus name I pray

Dear God

Today I went to revival and got my soul revived. Thank you Lord for the message that was brought forth tonight. I give you the honor and the glory for opening my mind to understand your word. Lord I ask you to bless the pastor, give him manner from on high to feed us nightly. Let the words of his mouth and the mediation of his heart be acceptable in your sight. Continue to bless Second Baptist Church and our pastor, George Waddles Jr. Bless those that are standing in the need of a blessing, let us continue to lean and depend on your word, Lord we can't make it without you. Lord I pray that you bless the sick and shut-in. Bless those that are grieving for their loved ones, forever hold them in the palm of your hand. Father let them know that weeping may endure for a night, but joy cometh in the morning. Lord let me continue to tell others that it's a good thing to show forth thy loving kindness in the morning and thy faithfulness every night. Lord continue to guide my footsteps as I walk this journey learning of you and your goodness towards me. Give me understanding and knowledge to learn of you, and share the love that I have for you with others that may not know just how great you are. Lord my prayer is that you will open up a window and pour your blessings down on countries that have been hit with so much devastation. Help them to know that you are about good and that they need to be faithful through the good times as well as the bad. To trust you and faint not. Let them know that when we are at our lowest, you are at your best, already working it out. Bless my house Lord, as we bless you. In Jesus name I pray Amen.

Kathleen Copeland

Dear God

I'm giving thanks for such loyal, kind, caring, and loving friends, Michael and Grace Sawyers. Lord Marvin and Myself are so grateful for having been blessed to have such great friends in our circle of friends. Father I know it's by your grace that you placed Michael in my husbands life, our destiny is all already planned out by you. Thank you for the ride or die friendship that these two have shared down through the years.

Nothing or nobody but you can separate the love that they share for one another. Lord we are so grateful for blessing Michael with a wife that loves him unconditionally. You blessed him with a strong woman with wonderful values. Continue to bless his family, hold his children and grandchildren in the palm of your hand, keeping them from hurt harm and danger. Heavenly Father when Michael is feeling weak, weary and torn, carry him until he can stand alone. Be the anchor that he needs when he's in pain, cover him with your love and blood of protection. Lord be his shield and buckler in all situations.

Bless Michael and Grace as they care for their parents, honoring them as you told us too. Lord bless our friend Michael as he cares for his Mother, let her days be pain free and joyful as she awaits your return. Lord Michael and Grace have impacted students lives from all across this world, continue to lead and guide their footsteps as they continue to help and influence our children. Keep them in good health and strength. Let their minds be open and receptive to helping those that are standing in the need.

Father let the light that shines within Michael and Grace be seen for many years to come. Knowing Lord that they were just pilgrims passing through this barren land trying to make a difference in someone's life. Father I'm thankful for my friend and the love he has for you, bless his life as he blesses you. I pray this prayer over the life of our special friends, The Sawyers Family and their families, as they raise and nurture little Akira's life, open up a window and pour her out a blessing that will be too much to receive. In Jesus name I pray, Amen.

Kathleen Copeland

Dear God

It's October 26, 2016 I'm screaming happy birthday to my second mom Mrs. Jones who fell asleep and is awaiting your return. Lord I miss the talks that we shared, she was such a great influence in my life. She believed in me, and wanted the best for me. Lord thank you for waking me up with a new mind and attitude. Continue to have your way and being God in every situation that I go through. When I make mistakes, please pick me up and turn me around place my feet back on solid ground. Forgive me for all of my sins, spoken and unspoken. Lord do not hold against us the sins of the past generations, may your mercy come quickly to meet us, for we are in desperate need. Lord continue to be my light and my salvation, the stronghold of my life. When trouble comes my way be my dwelling place, hide me in the shelter of your tabernacle and set me high upon a rock and I will forever give you the honor the glory and the praise. In Jesus name I pray Amen.

Dear God

Help me not to become polluted by this world, but to be about helping others who are in distress. Father let me be completely humble, patient and loving, making every effort to keep the unity of the spirit through the bond of peace. Help me to walk humbly and act justly in my walk with you. All that I am and all that I can be I Place in your hands, all my trials and troubles, my discomforts, my disappointments, I place in your hands. Lord I surrender it all to make my walk more intimate and more real with you. Lord I pray that I lead by example not by words but visible force, let the love that I have for you shine through me so that others can see the love that I have for you. Lord bless me to be strong and courageous, not terrified or discouraged whatever life takes me, knowing that where I am you already there. Forgive me for all my sins. Continue to bless and keep is in your will. In Jesus name I pray Amen.

Kathleen Copeland

Dear God

I've been listening to this song all night long, can't sleep, I've been in the storm too long. Lord to all those that feel like you've been in your storm long enough it's time to get up and get out the pathway of whatever has been holding you down. When life gets hard and rough that's when you look to the hills for your help, it's there and always has been just waiting on you to ask him to come and help you out the present situation that you are in. Father I've been in my storm for over a year, I got to move on, my Mom is not coming back to this Earth, my heart has hurt long enough, remove this storm from me Lord. My breakthrough came last night thank you Jesus, for being the on time God that you are. My burdens are light, my husband no longer needs to hold me until I fall asleep, I slept all night in your arms lord. Mom I love you, but I'm going to let you sleep in the arms of Jesus until he comes for the both of us. I will wrap myself in your blanket when I feel lonely and need to feel your presence. I'm finally going to be alright, my joy came this morning in the way of a song. Thank you Jesus, and thank you Pastor Bertrand Bailey Jr. In Jesus name I pray Amen.

Dear God

Giving thanks for another day that you have given me. Lord thanks for joy, peace and happiness that I have today. Continue to lead and guide my every steps through life. Forgive me for all my sins, if I have wronged anyone I pray that I will make it right. Bless my family, continue to keep them safe with your love and blood of protection. I pray for good health and strength for everyone. Bless those that don't know you, my prayer is that they get to hear and learn of the love that you have for all your children. Lord this world that we know is slowly coming to an end. I pray that you will receive me in your kingdom when you come, let everyone that knows you adhere to your words and trust that you are coming back soon to take us home to live eternally with you. There will be no more sickness, death, or sorrows, just peace and happiness for those that believe in you. Lord I pray that we shall be ready. In Jesus name I pray Amen.

Heavenly Father,

To those that may be feeling weary, weak and torn you said in your word," They that wait upon the Lord, shall renew their strength, they shall mount up on wings like an Eagle, they shall run and not get weary, they shall walk and not faint". Wait patiently I say on the Lord, be of good courage and he will direct your pathway, and make your future bright. Lord help them to know that weeping only endures for a night, but joy with belief will come in the morning. Soothe their aching hearts and restore their faith. I know that you can do all things for those that love and trust you. Help us today Lord I pray in Jesus name Amen.

Heavenly Father

I come before you on bended knees to tell you how much I love and adore you. Lord you mean so much to me and my family, thanks for being the light in my life and the source of my strength. You have been my shield and protector down through the years and I am so grateful. I give you total praise in all that I do. Lord I want to live so that I may dwell in your house forever, to see the beauty of your kingdom that you have prepared for those that love and abide by your word. Lord I ask that you continue to create in me a clean heart and a renewed spirit to live for you all the days of my life. I pray for those that don't know you, forgive us of our daily sins. In Jesus name I pray Amen.

Dear God,

I declare that all evil, confusion, hatred, envy and pride against one another will be dispelled, in the name of Jesus. I pray that we come together as a nation to serve one God before you return. Lord if we don't come together down here I know we won't make it to live with you in our new home that you have prepared for us. Lord I pray that the killing of each other will end, that hatred can be filled with love from this day forward. My prayer is that we can love our neighbors as we love ourselves, to treat everyone with kindness regardless of their race. My prayer is for world peace, in Jesus Name I pray Amen.

TESTIMONIAL

Dear God

I'm giving thanks that on today January 13, 2017 that you once again showed me grace and mercy. Lord the call that I got from the hospital saying I need to come back in because the results from my mammogram was not good, it threw me into prayer mode, I didn't ask why me just heal me and remove whatever it was that was there. My husband and I went down on our knees and began to pray, as we entered the hospital I still was praying and claiming victory in Jesus name, I was told that I would have 3D X-rays and a ultrasound. I prayed after and before the X-Rays, While the doctor read the X-rays I read psalms 27-34-36-37. I was told that I had three Cyst in one breast, and a lump in the other, I was praying that it wouldn't be cancer, the doctor read the tests and said no cancer, it didn't look good, but I asked you to fix it and you did, I'm grateful and thankful for your goodness and mercy shown towards me again. Lord I praise you, I lift your name on high, I give you all the glory. Thank you for your blessing Lord. I will keep seeking, asking, and knocking because I know you will answer and come see about your child.

Dear God,

I believe that you will do the impossible in my life. Lord I know you are able and I'm not worried, I walk in the newness of Christ. You are Jehovah Jireh, my provider.

Thanks for loving me when I didn't love myself. I plead the blood of Jesus against any forces of evil that cause me or my family members to speak, act and think out things that are not in conjunction with your will. Lord let me continue to be that woman that walks by faith, not by sight. I believe in amazing grace, that there's power in the blood. Thanks Lord for not being blind to my tears and never silent to my pain. You see, you hear and you delivers. Lord you said you would not cause pain without allowing something new to be born, Isaiah ch 66-9-. Thank you lord for your goodness. In Jesus name I pray Amen.

Heavenly Father

I come before you with a bowed down head and a humble heart thankful for another day that you allowed me to see. Lord I know it's your grace and mercy that has kept me, and I give you the honor and the glory for keeping me. Lord I have hidden your Word deep down in my heart, that I may not sin against you. I will meditate in your precepts, and have respect for your ways all the days of my life. Lord I know it's a good thing to give thanks unto you and to sing praises unto your name O most high, to show forth your loving kindness in the morning and thy faithfulness every night so that I may triumph in thy work that you have instructed me to do. Lord I pray for strength to tell others of your goodness and wondrous works. In Jesus name

Dear God,

Today my friend and neighbor got her wings to fly home to be with you. Lord i pray for strength for her two children who may not understand your ways. Hold them close when they are feeling lonely and missing their Mom. Bless her family and be with them during these difficult days. Lord help them to know that absent from the body is to be present with you. I pray for all those that are grieving the loss of a loved one. Lord help us to remember that this place is not our home, it's a holding station until you come in the clouds to take us to our permanent home that you have prepared for us, in your Father's house. God I will be steadfast, unmovable, unchangeable, always abounding in your work. In Jesus name I pray, Amen.

Dear God,

Today April 14, 2017 is Good Friday, thanks for Jesus dying on the Cross for a sinner such as I. Lord your only begotten Son laid down his life so that we may live again, and that is the greatest gift of Love that man could receive. There's no greater love than a man that would lay down his life for a friend. Thank you Jesus for staying in that grave for three days, and rising on that third day so that we to may rise up when you return. They hung you high, and stretched you wide, and you just hung your head and died, never saying a unkind word, only asking your Father to forgive them, now that's truly love. Lord I know you are in the Holy place preparing to come and receive those that have kept your commandments, I'm praying daily that my name is written in the Lambs Book of Life. I live daily for your return, and when I sin, please forgive me and place me back on solid ground. In Jesus name I pray, Amen.

Heavenly Father,

Let him who is struggling against the power of appetite look to the Savior in the wilderness of temptation. Let him see Jesus in his agony upon the cross. He has endured all that is possible for us to bear, his victory is ours. Lord, Jesus rested upon the wisdom and strength of you, his Father. As long as we are united to you God, by our Faith, sin has no more dominion over us. By every word that proceedeth out of the mouth of God, we are to live when temptation comes, look not to circumstances, or weakness of self, but to the power of the Word. All its strength is yours, thy word says the Psalmist, "have I hid in mine heart, that I might not sin against, thee". By the Word of thy lips I have kept me from the paths of the Destroyer. Psalm 119:11 -17:4. In Jesus name I pray Amen.

Heavenly Father

Thank you, for thinking that We was worth saving, you sacrificed your life for us so that we could be free, so that We could be whole, so that We could tell everyone that I know, how much you loved us, Lord thank you for being the good Shepherd that gave your life for the sheep. Had it not been for your Grace and Mercy we would not be here today. Lord I'm asking your blessings upon those that are grieving the loss of loved ones. Give us the strength that we need to make it through these difficult days ahead. Bless families that are been killed daily during war, and all acts of violence. Bless those that are fighting to keep us safe. Bless there family as well. In Jesus name I pray, Amen.

Lord

I am sojourner in the Earth for you, my soul breaketh for the longing of Your Word at all times. Lord I will keep telling my testimonies, because they are my delight and my counsellors. Lord my prayer is that you teach me thy statutes, make me understand the way of your precepts, so that I may meditate on your wondrous works. Strengthen me according unto thy word, give me understanding as well. Lord I'm leaning on your everlasting arms, hide me in your bosom till I want no more, mold me, hold me, make me more like you each and everyday as I strive to live a life that's pleasing in your sight. Lord let me continue to feast off of the Manna that's sent by you. In Jesus name I pray, Amen.

Heavenly Father,

I will delight myself in thee because you delighted in me. Isaiah 62:4. Lord I delight myself in thee, and I know that you will give me the desires of my heart, to love and obey your word daily. I will commit myself unto you Lord, I will trust in your Word, and you, knowing that you will bring it to pass. Forgive me for all sins, known and unknown. Lord I will rest in you and wait patiently on you to come see about your child. Lord I will cease from anger when I'm provoked. Help me be better than evildoers, because I know that they will be cut off. I want to live a life so that I will be able to witness you coming in the Clouds to receive those that have their names written in the Lamb's book of life. You said in your Word,"He that followeth after righteousness and mercy findeth life, righteousness, and honor. Proverbs 21:21. In Jesus name I pray Amen.

Dear God,

When I rose this morning I didn't have no doubt in my mind that it was because of your Grace and mercy towards me, that I'm here. Thank you Lord for all your blessings that you have given me. Thanks for your instructions on how we should live and follow you. Lord I have had some good days as well as some bad, but you have been my shield and buckler through my storms. Lord when I hit a stumbling block in life, help me to remember that something better is on the way, that setbacks are just comebacks for better and greater. As I travel this path called life, forever be with me in my endeavors to honor you. In Jesus name I pray Amen.

*Bread cast upon waters usually returns
to man, right when it's needed.*

Heavenly Father

I'm praying for our youth and young adults whose feeling weak, low, lost and torn. Lord I ask your blessings upon those that feel that death is their only option. Let them know that you are love, that they can come to you at anytime, day or night, you are never too busy to come and hear and listen to your child. I pray as parents that we teach our children from birth that they are loved, teach them about our Heavenly Father, and that his ways are not our ways. Let us tell them that they can come to you, when they feel like there's no one else that they can trust, that's there's no problem that you can't solve. Lord our children are standing in the need of a huge blessing, they need protection from the Evil thoughts that the Devil is putting in there heads and minds. Lord I'm praying as parents that we keep a close watch over our children, when something seems off or wrong, Lord step in and cover them with your blood and love of protection, especially when we can't. In Jesus name I pray Amen.

Dear God,

When the righteous cry out for help, thanks for hearing and delivering them from trouble, thanks for being near the broken hearted and saving those that are crushed in the spirit. Lord thanks for being in our lives and allowing us to call upon your Holy and righteous name. Your Word said, "come unto me, all that labor and are heavy laden and you will give us rest." In Jesus name. Amen.

Dear God,

Thanks for calling us your Child. You know that we need help and you are there like our parents to pick us up when we fall. You are truly my Rock and my Salvation, I fear no one because you are my strength in life. My entire life rests upon you Lord, my whole being depends on your love for me. Your Word is more precious than gold. Thanks for being patient with me during every step of my journey. My prayer is to be faithful every day of my life. In Jesus name. Amen.

Dear God,

You are my Light and my Strong Tower, with you, whom shall I fear, Lord you are the strength of my life, of whom shall I be afraid, when the wicked comes against me, my enemies and my foes, you made them stumble and fall. Thank you Lord, what a mighty God I serve. For in times of trouble you shall hide me, I shall be lifted up above my enemies. All we need is to believe that you can and you will deliver us from any and all situations. Lord I pray for faithfulness in all that I do to honor you. It's not about me, but you in all that I do. In Jesus name I pray, Amen.

Heavenly Father

Change me oh Lord, make me more like you, wash me through and through. Make me more like your image that I may worship you. Lord what's not like you on the inside of me, wash me white as snow, change my heart, my mind and soul to live for you all the days of my life. I know you can and I believe that you will fix whatever needs changing in my life, and others as well. I know with your Grace and mercy I'm not what I use to be, I'm not where I need to be, but I'm better than I was because of the changes that I made so far. I'm reaching for more and better, in my walk with you, continue to change me to be all that I can for you Lord. In Jesus name I pray. Amen.

Dear God,

I'm grateful that the dust shall return to Earth as it was and the Spirit shall return unto you who gave it. I know that the conclusion to life is to fear you and to keep your commandments which are the duties of Man. Lord I know you shall bring every work into your judgement, with every Secret thing whether it be good or evil, we must answer to. Bless me Father, for I am a Sinner saved by Grace. Amen.

Dear God,

The word is love, shown to us when you died on the cross for our sins. Thanks for loving us enough to die that we may live again with you in Heaven, if we confess with our mouth and believe in our hearts that you died

Rose up from the grave so that we too may get up when you come again. Lord I have hidden your word deep down in my heart, so that when the storms of life is raging in my life, I too can pull out the word that I had hidden in my heart so that I may not sin against you. Any situation that I get into Lord I know I can pull out a word and work it for my good and the good of them that love you. In Jesus name I pray Amen.

Dear God

So many times I hear people say, "I'll come to church when I get myself cleaned up, or when I get right, I'm here to tell you that there's not enough Bleach, Tide Washing Powder, or Oxi-Clean to wash you clean as you can Lord. Jesus you can and will remove all dirt from us, we only need to ask you, and you will forgive us of our sins, and cleanse us from all unrighteousness. Lord my prayer is that we all shall be washed white as Snow. In Jesus name I pray Amen.

Dear Lord,

I heard your Shepherd say that when you speak every tongue shall confess, black, white, or brown shall bow down, hatred, racism, alcoholism, drugs, and murdering will cease when you speaks. There will be no more division among us. Matthew chapter 8-5- tells us that we are healed just by your word, you cast devils out, just by speaking a word, thanks for the love.

You are awesome and worthy to be praised. Even the wind shall obey when you speak. I'm blessed and honored to serve you Lord. In Jesus name I pray Amen.

Dear God—

Lord the Word says, "do not fear any of those things which you are about to suffer, " the flooding in Texas, the killings that we are seeing daily, all the trials and tribulations that we are going through, all we need to do is be faithful unto death and you will give us a crown of life. When tragedy comes our way Lord you are the same today, yesterday and tomorrow. You hear our cries a lot more when we are in trouble. Thanks for never leaving us. My prayer is that we call upon you more than ever during these difficult times, in Jesus name I pray Amen.

Kathleen Copeland

A Love Letter

To God

Dear God,

When I fell in love, I didn't know it would feel so good, knowing I had

Found someone who loves me unconditionally, regardless of how many times I mess up, he would be right there, ready to forgive me, and to welcome me back

Into his loving arms. Falling in love with you Jesus is the best thing that I ever done. You woke me up every morning, you put food on my table, you blessed me with the use and activity of my limbs, you protects me from hurt, harm, and danger, I can't help but to love you. In your arms I feel so protected, never disconnected, you are my refuge and my fortress, no one has ever come to my

Rescue the way you have. Lord I love you because you gave your Angels instructions to watch over me and to keep me safe. Because you love me so much, when you call upon me I will answer, I will be with you and honor you all the days of my life. No one but you, could have so much love that you gave up your life that I may live, that's why I love you so much my prince of peace, my almighty God, my king of kings. I love you Lord. In Jesus name I pray Amen.

Dear God,

Please be merciful unto me, fighting, hatred, and killing each other is all around us. It oppresses me greatly to have to live in fear, this is not the life you planned for your children. You died on Calvary Cross that we may have life, and have it more abundantly. Lord I will trust in you,

Heavenly Father,

My soul is restless, my mind is consumed with the worries of the world, the hatred, and killing of each other daily for senseless reasons is so troubling. Lord we need you more than ever. I know you see my pain, you know my thoughts and you will answer and fix this mess of a world that we live in down here. Lord I know that you are not coming until the word has been spread to everyone, even those that are persecuting us daily. Give me strength to hang in there, and hold to your word that trouble won't last always. Lord cover us with your blood of protection. Lord help me to remain faithful to you, when I'm hurt, confused, and afraid. Lord I pray that evil for evil never enters my heart, if it does please forgive me. Where I'm weak, make me strong, when I fall, pick me up, when my days seems dark and dreary, give me sunny days. Sometimes I need a Blessed Assurance that you are with me at all times. In Jesus name I pray Amen.

Dear Lord,

I will worship you in the splendor of your holiness, tremble before you in all the Earth. You are my rock, my sword, and shield, you are a Wheel Lord in the middle of a wheel, I will love you with all my heart, mind, and soul until it's your time to call, and my time to answer. My divine purpose is to serve you and show loving kindness to all. Thank you Lord for the blessings that you have bestowed upon me over and over again. In Jesus name I pray Amen.

Dear God,

Thank you for Grace, I read that Grace is the power of you God, Lord I learned that your Grace is given to all, so that we may live right, Titus2-11.

Lord I pray that Grace saves us from our lawlessness, but not from the law.

Lord your Son Jesus the Christ says that until heaven and earth pass away, your law would remain forever. Thank you for the Law. In Jesus name I pray Amen.

Dear God,

2017 is coming to a end, my prayers is that you continue to shower down your blessings upon my family and others. Give is wisdom and strength to serve you in all that we do. Lord let the problems of 2017 not carry over to 2018. Give all that call upon your name a new start. Forgive me of all my sins, my desire is to be a better servant, a good wife and mother, a great grandmother and a Godly woman of God. Lord help me to say no to ungodly ways. Help me to continue to study your word and learn all that I can of your desires and your ways. Thank you for another wonderful year, thank you for the blessings to come if it's your will. Lord I just want to follow the Lamb. In Jesus name I pray, Amen.

Kathleen Copeland

Dear God,

My heart is heavy with grief, so many are falling asleep in your arms daily. I know death is not the end, but it hurts. Today my cousin got his wings, he's resting waiting on your return, give the family strength to accept your call. Lord I want to live a life that's pleasing to you, so that when you call I'll be ready to answer. Keep your arms of protection all around us. Lord keep us clothed in our right minds, let evil not overcome us. In all things I give you honor. In Jesus name I pray Amen.

Dear God,

It's 2018 another year that you have blessed me to see. I'm giving you thanks for life, my health, my family, friends, and enemies if there be some.

Lord I won't complain about my needs and wants, because I trust that you will give me the desires of my heart according to your riches in glory. Lord I'm grateful to be here, so many have fallen asleep to await your return. In your word Joshua 24:15 says,"choose you this day, whom you will serve, as for me and my house, we will serve you Lord all the days of our lives, so that we can live with you forever and ever. In Jesus name I pray Amen.

Dear God,

Please be merciful unto me, fighting, hatred, and killing is all around us. It oppresses me greatly having to live in fear daily. Lord I know that this is not the life you planned for your children. Lord I will put my trust in you, I will not fear what flesh can do to me, you already paid the ultimate sacrifice on the cross, you died so that we may have life and have it more abundantly. In the shadow of your wings will I make my refuge, until these days come to pass. In Jesus name I pray Amen.

Dear God,

Have mercy upon me, my family, my friends, and all the people that has asked me to pray for them. Lord blot out all of our transgressions, cleanse us from all unrighteousness, renew within us a right spirit. Restore unto us your spirit of salvation. Lord I ask that you hear my prayer according to your kindness and multitude of tender mercies. Lord I humble myself before you. Lord forgive us for our bitterness or anger towards anyone at this time. I pray that we see only the good in others and not judge. In Jesus name I pray Amen.

Dear God,

Time is winding up here on Earth, this world is getting more and more corrupt each day. Forgive me for all of my sins, known and unknown. Lord any negative or unkind word spoken from my lips, I ask you to forgive me. You said in your word, "that whosoever call upon your name, shall be delivered". I call upon you now, and pray that you set me free. I repent today Lord, in Jesus name I pray Amen.

Dear God,

My heart belongs to you, I'm trying to do your will, because I'm saved, filled with the precious gift of the Holy Spirit. Lord I find nothing but peace and joy in your word. My needs I know you will supply. Lord I surrender all of me to you. Every area of my life I give to you, I will go wherever you have me to go. I realize that my life is not my own, to you and only you I belong. I give myself to you. This place is not my home, I'm only here for a short time, then I will live with you forever. In Jesus name I pray Amen.

Kathleen Copeland

Dear Heavenly Father,

This morning I'm praying for my church family. Lord I'm praying that the spirit of love and holiness will prevail in the hearts of all those that are gathered in your house today. Let us feast off of the manna that is being fed to us today. Release an outpouring of your Holy Spirit from heaven today upon all flesh with the gifts of the Holy Ghost. Lord I pray that you break the power of darkness that seeks to hinder the flow of your Holy Spirit. We bind the works of the devil in Jesus name. Lord I pray a special prayer for our Pastor and his family, continue to strengthen him as he blesses us with your word. Lord let your power be manifested during our Sunday mornings worship service. In Jesus name I pray Amen.

Dear God,

    It's February 8ᵗʰ 2018, today is mom's birthday. Lord I need you to send your angels to watch over me today, to guide my feet, to give me a reason to go on. I'm feeling hurt, lost and sad. Lord I realize mom's in a better place than I am, but death hurts. I miss her smile and laughter. To honor your parents is a privilege given by you, so that our days may be long upon the earth. I pray that I honored both parents well. Lord bless my siblings as well, there hearts are heavy as well. Mom was our glue that keep this family together, she raised us to lean and depend on each other, to always show love for family, friends, and strangers. To treat others the way we would want to be treated. Strengthen the family as we share the memories of our dear Mother Annie Bell Clifton. In Jesus name I pray Amen.

Dear God,

Thank you for the spiritual blessings that you have given us in heavenly places, in Christ. Help us to stay Holy and without blame before you in love. Thanks Lord for having made known to us the mystery of your will in whom we have obtained inheritance, according to the purpose of him who worketh all things after your will. We give you glory in all that we do and say. Let not our hearts be troubled, but give us the desire to believe in you. Lord we acknowledge you In every task that we do, we lean not unto our own understanding, but in all our ways we surrender to your will and ways. In Jesus name I pray Amen.

Dear God,

I know when this life is ending there will come a time when we will choose which day we will serve you, the Sabbath or Sunday. Father I know there is none like you in all the Earth. You are God, all by yourself. Lord I believe in the fourth commandment, the Sabbath and to keep it Holy. You consulted no one in creating this earth, and I say thank you. Lord I worship you for who you are, and what you mean to me. Lord keep me in your will, as I try to be pleasing in your sight. Lord I pray that when you do come in the clouds of Glory that our flight be not in winter or on the Sabbath day. Forgive me for all of my sins, Lord I choose this day to forgive everyone and everything and to walk free from the death that unforgiveness brings. Lord increase me with wisdom and knowledge so that I can see your truth in every situation of my life. Thank you Lord for caring about every aspect and details of my life, fulfilling them as you see fit. Whatever it is you have called me to do in my life, now and in the future, I pray that you would grant me the serenity to accept the things that you have me do and give me courage to get them done, and done well. Lord I pray that my life be a testimony of the power of your glory as I strive to build and uplift your kingdom. In Jesus name I pray Amen.

Dear God,

I'm asking your blessings upon my aunts and uncle, Lord continue to bless and strengthen Laura, Mazie(cookie) and John(tommy). Lord please keep your arms of protection around my mothers sisters and brother. Protect their children and grandchildren from all hurt, harm and danger. Lord give them the desires of their hearts. Let their steps line up with your will and your ways. Lord bless their homes and finances, anything that's not pleasing in your sight remove. Let their walk be steadfast, unmovable, always abounding in your word. Lord I pray that you fill their hearts with love in the absence of their sister, mother and father. Lord my prayer is that you continue to cover and watch over my family with your blood that you shed on Calvary. In Jesus name I pray Amen.

Dear God,

It's no secret about what you can do, or what you have done for others, I know you will do the same for me to. With your arms opened wide, thank you for pardoning me for all that I have done. Your continued love for me and others I say thank you. Lord because of your love and mercy I'm wiser I'm better than better, I can walk through the fire as long as you are with me Lord. In Jesus name I pray Amen.

A One Woman's Play—God Who Am I

God, I need to talk to you, do you hear me God? I need to know who I am. I know that I was born of a woman, shaped and mold after your own heart, was I born to be a helper to man, or a servant to you. God I pray that I wasn't born to be a slave to man. God is it true that you created man and woman after your own image? God, in that book called Genesis it says that you took the rib from man's side and formed woman, is this the reason that a man leaves his mother and father to be joined to his wife. God who am I, I was born in a world of sin, only to be saved by your goodness and mercy, so am I a servant to you, I'm suppose to live a life that's pleasing in your sight. Tell me God, who am I. God how can i dream of heavenly things when I don't know about the earthly things.

God, is dreaming of nice things foolish, is it like chasing the wind, because all things are decided by fate, it was known long ago what each man or woman will be, if that's so, I know it's no arguing about my destiny, i am who you says I am. God tell me who I am so that I can be pleasing in your sight, I want to tackle whatever task you put before me. Lord I want to love you with all my heart, mind and soul, but first I need to know who I am. God, sometimes I think I'm the woman at the well, who left her water pots and went into the city and told the men to come, see a man that told me all things that ever I have done. God is that who I am? Sometimes God I feel like I'm Mary and Martha. I cried out to you when my Mother died, you didn't hear me, I wanted you to bring her back like you did Lazarus, why didn't you answer me God, wasn't I important enough. God you raised Jairus daughter, why not let my mom live. When Jesus was in a city called Nain, he saw a mother weeping for her son who had died and he was raised up at that moment. Who am I God? Are you listening to me, please answer me, aren't you supposed to give me the desires of my heart. Sometimes I feel like Mary, your Son's Mother, following Jesus unto death. I will honor and worship you all the days of my life, so that I may have eternal life with you forever and ever. God could I be the daughter of the king, the most high, born for a purpose to bring truth to the world, by telling others of your love and goodness for all.

God sometimes I feel like I'm Grace, Mercy, love, joy, peace, happiness, righteous, cherished, and treasured. God until I see you coming in the clouds, and until I hear the trumpet blow, can I just say that I'm one of your good and faithful servants, a laborer for my master, who has been working daily so that I may obtain eternal life with you. God I do know that I'm a woman that has been redeemed by the blood of the lamb, that walks by faith, not by sight. God i also know that you died one Friday, I know that you stayed in the grave all day Saturday, but early Sunday morning you rose up with all power in your hands, so that we too may rise when it's your time to call, and my time to answer your call. So God who am I?

Can I just say that I'm a Sinner saved by your Grace.

Dear God,

When you close a chapter in my life, I pray that I leave that book closed. If you closed that chapter in my life, I know it was because my greater is on the way. Re-opening that book in my life only sets me back further. Sometimes I feel like you speaks to me through my circumstances. I may not understand your will, but I trust your Word. Lord in making decisions, the hardest thing may not be in choosing good or bad, but choosing what's good or best. Lord my prayer is that I continue to search your Word, I know the answer is in the Scriptures. The Holy Spirit will reveal your plan for my life, help me to wait on a word from you. Be Blessed.

A Birthday Prayer
For Our Son
Marc Philip Copeland

Dear God

Today May 11th I'm screaming happy blessed birthday to our son Marc Philip Copeland. Lord thank you for allowing me to be apart of this young man's life. Marrying his dad and loving him as my own, has brought me nothing but joy. During his situations and struggles you kept him from hurt, harm, and danger. Thank you for keeping a hedge of protection all around him.

Lord you have blessed Marc with so much wisdom and knowledge beyond his years. You being an all knowing God saw the potential in our Son and you wouldn't let up on him, for that we are eternally grateful. Lord continue to bless his life, as he bless you. Keep that beautiful smile he wears so wonderfully on his face. My prayer is that he continues to grow and help others along the way.

Let his light shine within so that everyone he comes in contact with will know that he is truly sent by you. Heavenly Father bless his children, let the love flow from heart to heart. Keep them under your wings of protection at all times.

Lord I know their will be good days as well as bad, when the devil starts to run. Give him the strength to resist him, give him the words to tell that devil to flee from him, that he knows someone mightier than him, and his name is Jesus.

Lord continue to bless the relationship between a father and his son, let nothing or no one separate them from each other. Lord I pray that the love Marc has for his sisters and family will show others how to love, because you are love, joy, peace and happiness. Lord I pray that our Son will continue to be a blessing to you, to his family, his circle of friends, his children, to strangers that cross his path as well as himself. Heavenly Father I pray this prayer over the life of our son, Marc Philip Copeland, bless him with the desires of his heart and in all his ways to acknowledge you. In Jesus name we pray Amen.

Dear God

It's 11-4-2018

When darkness encompass all around me I will look to the hills for strength.

My strength comes from you Lord, who made the heavens and the earth. Lord as I bare the toils of life, pain and grief, bless me to be able to stand. My prayer is that you make me a better me for you. Lord shed light in my life where there's darkness, let your light so shine within me, so others may see your works. In the midst of my sorrow, I pray that I will continue to be faithful until death. Lord please continue to shield me from hurt harm and danger, as I wait upon you, renew a right spirit in me, let me mount back up with wings as a Eagle, help me to run and not get weary, to be able to walk and not get tired. Lord give me the strength to show forth my loving kindness to you every morning and be faithful every night. Heavenly Father, I ask your blessings upon everyone that are going through storms in their lives. Let us wait on you, being of good courage and cheer, you will fix us after awhile. In Jesus name I pray Amen.

Katy's book of
inspirational prayers

Kathleen Copeland — Author